I0475775

- 1 -

FEDERAL BUREAU OF INVESTIGATION

Date of transcription _____1/21/94_____

      THRISTA ROUSE, Indian female, date of birth May 21,
year not known, but believed to be approximately age eight, and
in the second grade of elementary school, was interviewed at the
residence of DONNA JORDAN, Route 1, Box 97, Elk Point,
South Dakota, telephone number (605) 966-5336. Present for the
interview was JEAN BROCK, DONNA JORDAN, DAN HUDSPETH, and Special
Agent (SA) WILLIAM VAN ROE. DAN HUDSPETH, Criminal Investigator
(CI), Bureau of Indian Affairs (BIA), told THRISTA the identities
of the interviewing CI and SA of the FBI, and the nature of the
interview. HUDSPETH explained to THRISTA the importance of this
matter and the fact that it was very important for her to tell
the truth. HUDSPETH spent a considerable amount of time with
THRISTA to determine if she knew the difference between a lie and
being truthful. Several examples were given and after it was
determined that THRISTA clearly knew the difference between a lie
and being truthful, the interview began. She explained that she
had moved to her grandmother's, ROSEMARY ROUSE's residence in
Marty, South Dakota, approximately two years ago and that her
grandmother is a good person. Since being in DONNA JORDAN's
house, she has told DONNA some things that had happened while she
was at her grandmother's. It was established that THRISTA used
the term "private parts" for the personal areas of her body. At
that point, HUDSPETH showed THRISTA a drawing of a young male
depicting the complete male torso. She then explained that her
Uncle GARFIELD had stuck his "private part" in her private part
in the front of her body. Uncle GARFIELD did this at her
grandmother's residence in a room where MELODY sleeps. She never
told her grandmother as she was scared. She believes this
incident occurred recently and may have been only a few days or
weeks prior to the interview. In the house at the time that this
occurred were also JESSIE and DESMOND and that JESSIE and DESMOND
did this also to ~~MELONEY~~ (~~phonetic~~) and TABATHA (~~phonetic~~).
JESSIE and DESMOND were doing the same things to ~~MELONEY~~ and
TABATHA when GARFIELD was doing it to her. At this time,
GARFIELD was drinking. She believes it was a weekend and it was
night time, about supper time, and that her grandmother and mom
had gone to town. Her mother is URSULA.

[handwritten margin notes: Melanie (left margin), Melanie (right margin)]

Investigation on ___1/19/94___ at ___Elk Point, SD___ File # ___198F-MP-39729___

by ___SA WILLIAM VAN ROE:smi___ Date dictated ___1/20/94___

JESSIE and DESMOND were also drinking. All the other children were in the house, but JESSIE locked them in a closet.

GARFIELD left his clothes on, but pulled his pants down or off and she was on the bed at the time and was tied up with brown colored rope. Her hands were tied away from her body and the ropes were tied to the bedposts. GARFIELD also tied her legs together and he tied her up before he pulled his clothes off/or pants down. GARFIELD had placed her on the bed on her stomach, face down, and he tried to put his private part/penis in her butt, but her grandmother came home before he could do it.

DESMOND and JESSIE did the same thing to her as GARFIELD had done. When DESMOND did it, it was in the same room, but it was a different day, and it actually occurred before GARFIELD had done it to her. This happened about one week before GARFIELD did it to her and she believes it was on a weekend. She was alone in the house with DESMOND and her mother was not at home and neither was her grandmother. JESSIE and GARFIELD had left the house and DESMOND locked the rest of the kids up in the closet. She had her clothes on, but DESMOND took her panties off. He had his pants pulled down and had his "private part"/penis out. She was tied up just like the other time. She recalled that his private part/penis was stiff and that DESMOND put his private part/penis in her private part in her front. She remembered that it hurt while he was doing it and that he did it "real fast." On this occasion, she was on the bed, looking up at the ceiling, and her legs were tied together. DESMOND got on top of her and moved his body up and down and she felt a "sticky" substance in her private part. After he was finished, he untied her and let her go, and she was scared and afraid that he would hurt her.

Her Uncle JESSIE did the same thing to her as DESMOND and GARFIELD and that Uncle JESSIE did it to her in the same room and that Uncle JESSIE did it to her sometime after DESMOND and GARFIELD had done it. She was alone with JESSIE and JESSIE tied her up and put his "private part"/penis in her butt and that it hurt. Again she was tied up and her legs were tied together and he kissed her while he was doing this to her. When he did this to her she felt "bad." After JESSIE was finished he told her, "Tell anyone and I will do it again to you." DONOVAN tried to help her when JESSIE was doing this to her, but JESSIE locked him in the closet.

Hubbeling

        She recalled that RUSSELL ~~HUDMAN~~ (phonetic) had moved,
but when he was around Marty, he put his "private part" in
ECKO's and FURY's butts. He also put his "private part" in her
butt too. HUDMAN did this to her about the same time that the
other men did it to her. She thought it was in the same time
frame, but it was after JESSIE had done it to her. She was in a
room in the house alone with RUSSELL and home at the time, in
addition to RUSSELL, was DESMOND, JESSIE, and GARFIELD. They had
all been drinking and no other adults were in the house and the
kids had all been locked in the closet. Her grandmother had left
the residence.

        HUDMAN put his "private part"/penis in her front
private part and when he did that his "private part" was hard.
When he did this to her she was tied up in MELODY's room and that
HUDMAN also tried to kiss her on her lips. HUDMAN told her,
"Don't tell or I'll do it again." When HUDMAN did this to her,
he had his clothes on, but his pants pulled down.

        She also recalled that DESMOND held FURY and JESSIE put
his "private part"/penis in her "private part" in her front. No
one else was home at the time and when DESMOND and JESSIE did
this to FURY it was approximately the same time that the others
did it to her. This occasion she thought was possibly a week or
so ago from the time of this interview and it was a weekday, it
was night time. When JESSIE did this to FURY, his "private
part"/penis was hard. She was a witness to this act that DESMOND
and JESSIE did to FURY.

        She believes that her mother has tried to help her and
pointed out that her mother knows what was happening to the
children.

        DESMOND, GARFIELD, and JESSIE made her smoke pot and
she described the feeling after smoking the pot as being "dumb."
They made her smoke pot about the same time that they did the
other things to her.

        Her grandmother broke a TV because she got mad at
GARFIELD and DESMOND for what they were doing to the children.

-1-

FEDERAL BUREAU OF INVESTIGATION

Date of transcription _____1/25/94_____

        THRISTA ROUSE, Indian female, was interviewed in the
Office of the United States Attorney, Sioux Falls, South Dakota.
Present for the interview was Assistant United States Attorney
(AUSA) MICHELLE TAPKEN and Bureau of Indian Affairs (BIA)
Criminal Investigator (CI) DAN HUDSPETH. THRISTA advised that
presently the lock has been broken off of the closet that was
used by her uncles to lock she and the other children in.
DERRICK broke the lock off the closet and currently there is no
lock on that particular closet. The closet is located in her
grandmother's home in Marty, South Dakota.

Investigation on __1/21/94__ at _Sioux Falls, SD_____ File # _198F-MP-39729_

by _SA WILLIAM VAN ROE:smi_____ Date dictated _1/24/94_____

FD-302 (Rev. 3-10—82)

- 1 -

FEDERAL BUREAU OF INVESTIGATION

Date of transcription   3/30/94

    THRISTA ROUSE appeared at the United States Attorney's Office to clarify statements that she had made about her uncles on a previous interview. She was interviewed in the presence of Special Agent (SA) WILLIAM VAN ROE of the FBI, and Assistant United States Attorney (AUSA) MICHELLE TAPKEN. ROUSE advised that GARFIELD FEATHER put his "private spot" into her "private spot." He also tried to put his "private spot" in her butt.

    DESMOND ROUSE put his "private spot" into her "private spot."

    JESSE ROUSE put his "private spot" in her front and butt.

    DESMOND ROUSE hurt the babies ECHO and FURY. He put his "private spot" in both their butts.

    RUSSELL HUBBELING hurt both the babies, ECHO and FURY. She saw him put his "private spot" in FURY's butt and also ECHO's butt.

Investigation on   3/21/94   at Sioux Falls, SD   File # 198F-MP-39729

by   SA WILLIAM VAN ROE:smi   Date dictated 3/24/94

- 1 -

FEDERAL BUREAU OF INVESTIGATION

Date of transcription   1/21/94

      LICREATIA ROUSE, Indian female, age six, and date of birth unknown, was interviewed at the residence of DONNA JORDAN, Route 1, Box 97, Elk Point, South Dakota, telephone number (605) 966-5336. LICREATIA advised that her mother is BEATA.

      The interview was conducted by Bureau of Indian Affairs (BIA) Criminal Investigator (CI) DAN HUDSPETH. HUDSPETH told LICREATIA the identities of the interviewing officers and that the matter was important. He explained that she needed to be truthful, spent a considerable amount of time explaining the difference between telling the truth and telling a lie, and numerous examples were given to LICREATIA and she readily displayed knowledge of the difference between lies and truthfulness. HUDSPETH also talked to LICREATIA about "good touches" and "bad touches." HUDSPETH then asked LICREATIA if anyone touched her in a bad way. She said that DESMOND ROUSE had put his hands between her legs and because of this she got angry. She explained that she knocked him off of her and at the time she had some of her clothing off and that his clothing was on. As a result of this incident with DESMOND, she fell off the bed and wet her pants.

      At the time of the incident her mother, BEATA, and her grandmother, ROSEMARY, were in the house.

      She also explained that her uncle DWAYNE ROUSE tried to touch her between her legs, but that she woke up.

      The incidents took place in the residence of ROSEMARY ROUSE in Marty, South Dakota.

Investigation on   1/19/94   at Elk Point, SD   File #   198F-MP-39729

by   SA WILLIAM VAN ROE:smi   Date dictated   1/20/94

- 1 -

FEDERAL BUREAU OF INVESTIGATION

Date of transcription   1/25/94

       LICREATIA ROUSE, Indian female, age six, was re-interviewed in the Office of the United States Attorney, Sioux Falls, South Dakota. Present for the interview was Assistant United States Attorney (AUSA) MICHELLE TAPKEN and Bureau of Indian Affairs (BIA) Criminal Investigator (CI) DAN HUDSPETH. ROUSE provided the following information:

       BEATA is her mother.

       The identities of the interviewing individuals were discussed with LICREATIA and the importance of telling the truth was discussed. LICREATIA advised she has been living at Marty, South Dakota, with her grandmother in her grandmother's house which she described as being blue in color. She moved to her grandmother's house just a few days ago and she described her grandmother as a good person.

       She explained that the following individuals also come to her grandmother's house:

       DESMOND, JESSIE, GARFIELD, RUSSELL, BEATA, her mother; URSULA, BOB, DWAYNE.

       DESMOND, GARFIELD, DWAYNE and JESSIE all drink at her grandmother's house.

       Good touches/bad touches were discussed and through discussion it was determined that LICREATIA understood the difference between a good touch and a bad touch. She explained that her uncles touch her mother in a bad way and that she told them not to touch her mother that way because her mother's body was hers and should not be touched that way.

       "Private parts" were discussed and LICREATIA stated that no one should touch "your private parts." She advised that individuals had done some naughty things to her and stated that the bruises that were found when she was examined by the doctor

---

Investigation on   1/21/94   at Sioux Falls, SD   File # 198F-MP-39729

by   SA WILLIAM VAN ROE:smi   Date dictated 1/24/94

were caused from her uncles and the bruises were on her "bottom."
She is afraid of her uncles and explained that she has bruises
where she "pee-pees." DESMOND put his hand in where she pee-pees
and pointed out that he used his middle finger when he did this.

A diagram of a male was shown to LICREATIA and she
described a man's penis as a "pee-pee," and pointed out this was
not used on her, but only DESMOND used his finger. She recalled
that when DESMOND did this to her that it hurt. She is afraid of
DESMOND and described DESMOND as an individual who drinks.

DESMOND told her that she could not tell what had
happened and she said she told DESMOND that she could tell and
that she did tell her mother.

JESSIE also puts his finger in her "peach" and she
described this as the area between her legs where she pee-pees.

She recalled that when JESSIE did this, her grandmother
woke up and slapped JESSIE. This incident happened approximately
one week ago which was after Christmas, and while she was six
years of age. She also recalled that her mother got mad over
this incident.

DWAYNE also tried to touch her, just like DESMOND did,
but she woke up.

D-502 (Rev. 3-10-82)

FEDERAL BUREAU OF INVESTIGATION `

Date of transcription ___1/25/94___

JESSICA ROUSE, Indian female, age four, was interviewed in the office of the United States Attorney, Sioux Falls, South Dakota. Present was Assistant United States Attorney (AUSA) MICHELLE TAPKEN and Bureau of Indian Affairs (BIA) Criminal Investigator (CI) DAN HUDSPETH. ROUSE advised that her mother was BEATA and her father is ART MEDICINE HORN. She lived at her grandmother's residence in Marty, South Dakota, the residence of ROSEMARY ROUSE, who she described as a good person. Her grandmother drinks whiskey, beer, gets drunk, and falls off the chair. Her grandmother's house is blue in color and at the present time they live in their own house. Her grandmother kicked she and her mother out of the grandmother's house and a short time ago the grandmother was drunk.

Also living at her grandmother's house at that time that she lived there were the following individuals:

Uncle JESSIE; DWAYNE; BOBO, whom she described as an aunt; her mother BEATA; DESMOND; GARFIELD; "TWIST".

These individuals all party, drink, smoke cigarettes which smell funny and make her eyes burn.

It was explained to JESSICA that it was important to tell the truth and a discussion ensued between what telling the truth was and what telling a lie was. She stated she understood the difference.

In addition, good touch/bad touches were discussed and it was obvious that she knew the difference between a good touch and a bad touch.

She explained that her Uncle JESSIE put his "private part"/penis in her pee-pee and when he did that it hurt. She cried and does not want him to do that again. This happened at her grandmother's when she spent the night in MELODY's room.

Investigation on 2|
1/19/94   at Sioux Falls, SD   File # 198F-MP-39729

by ___SA WILLIAM VAN ROE:smi___   Date dictated 1/24/94

That room has a door on it and the room is back by a closet. No
one else was in the room at the time, only she and Uncle JESSIE.

        DESMOND also did the same thing to her and he also did
it to the other kids. JESSICA explained that DESMOND "did bad
things." She explained that DESMOND put something in her where
she pees and the thing that he put in her was the thing that he
uses to pee with.

        She is afraid someone will hurt her if she tells what
happened to her and what happened to the other children. DERRICK
told her not to tell. She thought something bad would happen if
she did tell what had happened to her.

        She also explained that things also happened to
LICREATIA.

FD-302 (Rev. 3-10—82)

FEDERAL BUREAU OF INVESTIGATION

Date of transcription _____1/25/94_____

ROSEMARY ROUSE was re-interviewed at the Office of the
United States Attorney, Sioux Falls, South Dakota. Present was
Assistant United States Attorney (AUSA) MICHELLE TAPKEN and
Bureau of Indian Affairs (BIA) Criminal Investigator (CI) DAN
HUDSPETH.

ROSEMARY advised that the closet that her uncles used
to lock the children in which is located in her grandmother's
house in Marty, South Dakota, is in BEATA's room, and the lock
was on the outside of the door.

Investigation on __1/21/94__ at _Sioux Falls, SD_ File # _198F-MP-39729_

by __SA WILLIAM VAN ROE:smi__ Date dictated _1/24/94_

FD-302 (Rev. 3-10-82)

FEDERAL BUREAU OF INVESTIGATION

Date of transcription   1/25/94

     ROSEMARY ROUSE was re-interviewed at the Office of the United States Attorney, Sioux Falls, South Dakota. Present was Assistant United States Attorney (AUSA) MICHELLE TAPKEN and Bureau of Indian Affairs (BIA) Criminal Investigator (CI) DAN HUDSPETH.

     ROSEMARY advised that the closet that her uncles used to lock the children in which is located in her grandmother's house in Marty, South Dakota, is in BEATA's room, and the lock was on the outside of the door.

Investigation on   1/21/94   at Sioux Falls, SD   File # 198F-MP-39729

by   SA WILLIAM VAN ROE:smi   Date dictated 1/24/94

FD-302 (Rev. 3-10-82)

-1-

FEDERAL BUREAU OF INVESTIGATION

Date of transcription   1/25/94

     THRISTA ROUSE, Indian female, was interviewed in the
Office of the United States Attorney, Sioux Falls, South Dakota.
Present for the interview was Assistant United States Attorney
(AUSA) MICHELLE TAPKEN and Bureau of Indian Affairs (BIA)
Criminal Investigator (CI) DAN HUDSPETH. THRISTA advised that
presently the lock has been broken off of the closet that was
used by her uncles to lock she and the other children in.
DERRICK broke the lock off the closet and currently there is no
lock on that particular closet. The closet is located in her
grandmother's home in Marty, South Dakota.

Investigation on   1/21/94   at Sioux Falls, SD   File # 198F-MP-39729

by   SA WILLIAM VAN ROE:smi   Date dictated 1/24/94

FD-302 (Rev. 3-10-82)

FEDERAL BUREAU OF INVESTIGATION

Date of transcription   1/25/94

      JESSICA ROUSE, Indian female, age four, was interviewed in the office of the United States Attorney, Sioux Falls, South Dakota. Present was Assistant United States Attorney (AUSA) MICHELLE TAPKEN and Bureau of Indian Affairs (BIA) Criminal Investigator (CI) DAN HUDSPETH. ROUSE advised that her mother was BEATA and her father is ART MEDICINE HORN. She lived at her grandmother's residence in Marty, South Dakota, the residence of ROSEMARY ROUSE, who she described as a good person. Her grandmother drinks whiskey, beer, gets drunk, and falls off the chair. Her grandmother's house is blue in color and at the present time they live in their own house. Her grandmother kicked she and her mother out of the grandmother's house and a short time ago the grandmother was drunk.

      Also living at her grandmother's house at that time that she lived there were the following individuals:

      Uncle JESSIE; DWAYNE; BOBO, whom she described as an aunt; her mother BEATA; DESMOND; GARFIELD; "TWIST".

      These individuals all party, drink, smoke cigarettes which smell funny and make her eyes burn.

      It was explained to JESSICA that it was important to tell the truth and a discussion ensued between what telling the truth was and what telling a lie was. She stated she understood the difference.

      In addition, good touch/bad touches were discussed and it was obvious that she knew the difference between a good touch and a bad touch.

      She explained that her Uncle JESSIE put his "private part"/penis in her pee-pee and when he did that it hurt. She cried and does not want him to do that again. This happened at her grandmother's when she spent the night in MELODY's room.

Investigation on   1/21/94   at Sioux Falls, SD   File # 198F-MP-39729

by   SA WILLIAM VAN ROE:smi   Date dictated 1/24/94

198F-MP-39729

ontinuation of FD-302 of _JESSICA ROUSE_____, On __1/12/94___, Page __2__

That room has a door on it and the room is back by a closet. No one else was in the room at the time, only she and Uncle JESSIE.

DESMOND also did the same thing to her and he also did it to the other kids. JESSICA explained that DESMOND "did bad things." She explained that DESMOND put something in her where she pees and the thing that he put in her was the thing that he uses to pee with.

She is afraid someone will hurt her if she tells what happened to her and what happened to the other children. DERRICK told her not to tell. She thought something bad would happen if she did tell what had happened to her.

She also explained that things also happened to LICREATIA.

FEDERAL BUREAU OF INVESTIGATION

Date of transcription _____1/31/94_____

GARFIELD JUDE FEATHER, Indian male American, was interviewed at the residence of BEATA ROUSE, house number 515 East Indian Housing, Marty, South Dakota, on the Yankton Sioux Indian Reservation. FEATHER was told the identity of the interviewing Agent and the nature of the interview, as it pertained to sexual abuse allegations of children at the ROSEMARY ROUSE house, Marty, South Dakota. FEATHER advised that he had no idea that any of the children at the ROSEMARY ROUSE house had been abused. He has never seen anyone abuse the children in that house and could provide no information concerning DESMOND, DUANE, JESSE, RUSSELL HUBBELING or TONY SCHUNK abusing any children at that residence.

He has been away from the Marty area for a few years and only returned in October of 1993. He moved back to Marty from Aberdeen, South Dakota, where he was staying with his father.

He could provide no information concerning any of the children being tied up to beds or being placed and locked in closets.

He could provide no information concerning anyone abusing two babies, ECHO and FURY.

He admitted that a lot of drinking goes on in the ROSEMARY ROUSE house but no one abused the kids and everyone makes sure that they are fed and that they have clean clothes.

He advised that he would readily agree to take a polygraph and denied doing anything to hurt the children, especially THRISTA, ROSEMARY, LICREATIA, or JESSICA.

GARFIELD JUDE FEATHER is describes as an Indian male American; date of birth March 26, 1963; place of birth Wagner, South Dakota; 6 feet tall; 145 pounds; red hair; hazel eyes; facial characteristics - mustache; single; Social Security

Investigation on __1/25/94__ at __Marty, SD__ File # __198F-MP-39729__

by __SA WILLIAM VAN ROE/WVR:dmr__ Date dictated __1/27/94__

Account Number 504-70-7063; no military; GED diploma; no previous arrests; residing at the ROSEMARY ROSE residence, Marty, South Dakota, or with DEBBIE RAYMOND, his sister, Greenwood, South Dakota; children - ERICA FEATHER, age ten and one son, ANTHONY EAGLE, age nine; alias - GARFIELD RAYMOND; mother - ELIZABETH RAYMOND, Minneapolis, Minnesota, 208 Sixteenth Avenue South; father - JOHN FEATHER, Aberdeen, South Dakota, who works for the casino in Watertown, South Dakota; seven brothers and eight sisters.

FD-302 (Rev. 3-10-82)

- 1 -

FEDERAL BUREAU OF INVESTIGATION

Date of transcription _____3/30/94_____

    At approximately 8:45 a.m., GARFIELD JUDE FEATHER, Indian male, date of birth 3/26/63, was arrested without incident at the home of Rosemary Rouse, Marty, South Dakota. He was then transported to the Charles Mix County Law Enforcement Center where he arrived at approximately 9:12 a.m.

Investigation on _____3/30/94_____ at _Marty, South Dakota_ File #. _198F-MP-39729_

    SA ALFRED D. BRAMUCCI

by _SA DEAN A. SCHEIDLER:das_ Date dictated _3/30/94_

FD-302 (Rev. 3-10-82)

FEDERAL BUREAU OF INVESTIGATION

Date of transcription   1/31/94

RUSSELL DUANE HUBBELING, Indian male American, was interviewed at the residence of BEATA ROUSE, house number 515 East Indian Housing, Marty, South Dakota, on the Yankton Sioux Indian Reservation. HUBBELING was told the identity of the interviewing Agent and the nature of the interview, as it pertained to allegations of sexual abuse of children in the residence of ROSEMARY ROUSE. HUBBELING advised that he spends a great deal of time at ROSEMARY ROUSE's residence in Marty, South Dakota, and that there are numerous children also staying at that house. The children are all happy and he could provide no information concerning any sexual abuse of the children by anyone. All the people staying at the house have a good time including the children and the adults and they all watch a great deal of television and drink.

He could provide no information concerning anyone locking children in a closet or tying them up with ropes or sexually abusing them. He explained that "the family doesn't do things like abusing kids."

He denied that the children ever said anything to him about anyone abusing them and he vehemently denied abusing any of the children in the house. He specifically, when asked about TRISTA, ROSEMARY, ECHO and FURY, denied any wrongdoing and pointed out that these children are his nieces.

When confronted with the information that the children were implicating him in sexual wrongdoing he explained that he did not think the kids would say anything like that about him.

He denied that JESSE, DUANE, GARFIELD, or DESMOND had ever done anything to hurt or sexually abuse the children of that residence.

He has been in Eagle Butte, South Dakota, staying with his mother for approximately three weeks and just returned to Marty, South Dakota.

Investigation on   1/25/94   at Marty, SD   File # 198F-MP-39729

by _ SA WILLIAM VAN ROE/WVR:dmr   Date dictated 1/27/94

He does not think the adults in the family know anything about the sexual abuse charges.

His nieces and nephews are good children and he pointed out that, "the kids don't lie."

If there is anything wrong with the family he explained that "the family just parties too much."

When asked about a polygraph examination, HUBBELING advised that he would refuse to take a polygraph examination. At the time of the interview, HUBBELING appeared to be intoxicated.

RUSSELL DUANE HUBBELING is described as an Indian male American; date of birth August 12, 1964; place of birth Wagner, South Dakota; 6 feet tall; 200 pounds; brown hair; brown eyes; received GED; no military; single; no permanent address but spends a considerable amount of time at ROSEMARY ROUSE's residence, Marty, South Dakota, and the residence of BEATA ROUSE in Marty; Social Security Account Number 504-82-3604; South Dakota Driver's License - unknown; mother - BLOSSOM HUBBELING, Eagle Butte, South Dakota; aunt - ROSEMARY, Marty, South Dakota; father - DUANE (Deceased); cousins - JESSE ROUSE, DUANE ROUSE, BEATA ROUSE, DESMOND ROUSE, GARFIELD FEATHER, and TONY SCHUNK (close friend).

- 1 -

FEDERAL BUREAU OF INVESTIGATION

Date of transcription   4/6/94

     At 9:16 AM, RUSSELL DUANE HUBBELING, Native American male, date of birth August 12, 1964, was arrested without incident at his mother's residence located approximately two miles north and two miles west of Marty, South Dakota, on the Yankton Sioux Indian Reservation. HUBBELING was transported to the Charles Mix County Jail, Lake Andes, South Dakota, arriving at that facility at 9:30 AM.

     No questions were asked of HUBBELING from the time of the arrest until he arrived at the Charles Mix County Jail.

     Arriving at the Charles Mix County Jail, HUBBELING was presented one copy of Interrogation; Advice of Rights form which Special Agent (SA) VAN ROE read aloud to him. HUBBELING stated he understood his rights as read, signed the waiver portion of the form, and advised that he wished not to provide any information concerning this matter. The interview was immediately terminated.

     Bureau of Indian Affairs (BIA) Criminal Investigator (CI) DAN HUDSPETH accompanied SA VAN ROE when HUBBELING was arrested and transported to the Charles Mix County Jail.

Investigation on   3/30/94   at Marty, SD   File # 198F-MP-39729

by SA WILLIAM VAN ROE:smi   Date dictated 3/31/94

PD-302 (Rev. 3-10-82)

- 1 -

FEDERAL BUREAU OF INVESTIGATION

Date of transcription   1/28/94

        At 4:21 p.m. on January 25, 1994, DESMOND BENEDICT
ROUSE, also known as Dez Rouse, male American Indian, date of
birth September 5, 1964, was contacted at the Charles Mix County
Sheriff's Office, Lake Andes, South Dakota. He was advised of
the identities of the interviewing Agents and nature of the
interview. It should be noted that ROUSE confirmed he had
voluntarily come to the sheriff's office at the request of Bureau
of Indian Affairs (BIA) Criminal Investigator DAN HUDSPETH.
HUDSPETH had contacted ROUSE at the home of CLEO TAIL and
transported ROUSE to the sheriff's office.

        At the outset of the interview ROUSE was advised that
he was not under arrest and that the FBI had no intention of
arresting him at the conclusion of the interview. Further, he
was advised he did not have to answer any questions, but that if
he chose to do so he could stop answering questions and terminate
the interview at any time. He indicated he understood those
facts. ROUSE was further advised that he was free to go at any
time. ROUSE advised that he was sober and not under the
influence of any drugs or medications. He indicated he was
feeling well and that English was his best language.

        To ensure that he understood his rights, ROUSE was then
advised of his rights as they appear on an Interrogation; Advice
of Rights form. The form was read aloud to ROUSE while he
followed along, reading the form. ROUSE indicated he was willing
to participate in an interview and, following the reading of the
Waiver of Rights portion of the form, signed said form and the
interview then proceeded.

        ROUSE was then advised again of the nature of the
interview, that being concerning his alleged sexual abuse of
numerous children residing in his mother's house, that of
ROSEMARY ROUSE, in East Marty Housing, Marty, South Dakota. When
questioned, specifically, concerning whether he had touched the
groin area of LUCRITIA ROUSE, his niece, ROUSE replied,
"Probably, yeah." It should be noted he replied in that fashion

---

Investigation on   1/25/94   at Lake Andes, South Dakota File # 198F-MP-39729

        SA WILLIAM VAN ROE
by SA PAUL S. PRITCHARD:PSP:phs   Date dictated 1/27/94

198F-MP-39729

Continuation of FD-302 of ___DESMOND BENEDICT ROUSE_____ , on ___1/25/94___ , Page ___2___

twice, stating, "Probably, yeah." when asked if he had touched
LUCRITIA in her groin area. When asked to clarify when, where in
the house, and why he had touched her, ROUSE then claimed he
"didn't know," and further that "nothing happened." ROUSE
advised LUCRITIA lived in the same house as he did until she
moved out around the end of December, 1993. He advised she had
lived there since June or July.

ROUSE advised that he drinks a lot and gets drunk.
ROUSE stated, "I admit I have a drinking problem." He advised
that his brother JESSE ROUSE, and GARFIELD FEATHER also drink a
lot and get drunk.

ROUSE claimed he loved and cared about the children
living in his mother's house. He indicated that he believed the
children also loved and cared about him. ROUSE then volunteered
that he had kissed PRAIRIE ROSE ROUSE on the lips when she was
leaving his house. He claimed that was the only sexual act he
had with any of the children. ROUSE then advised that he passed
out a lot and "nothing could have happened cause JESS and
GARFIELD" were there, as well as others, and they were always
partying.

Upon further questioning concerning his relationship
with the children in the house, ROUSE asked, "What's the best
bet, should I get a lawyer?" ROUSE was informed that was
entirely up to him, but that if he wanted an attorney the
interview would stop immediately. He was then asked if he wanted
an attorney or if he wanted to continue the interview now,
without a lawyer present. ROUSE replied, "Yeah." When asked to
clarify his desires, ROUSE stated, "Do it now." The interview
then proceeded. It should be noted at 4:45 p.m. ROUSE smoked a
cigarette. At 5:23 p.m. he asked for a drink of water and left
the interview room unescorted, returning shortly thereafter.
ROUSE then asked, "What if I want to talk to a lawyer?" It was
again explained to ROUSE that that was his choice and that if he
wanted a lawyer the interview would be stopped immediately. At
5:26 p.m. ROUSE stated, "I want to talk to a lawyer." The
interview was then terminated. The interviewing Agents then got
up and started packing up notes and putting on coats. ROUSE then
stated, "Is it too late to change my mind?" ROUSE was advised
that since he had asked for an attorney, the interview had to be
stopped. He was advised that if he wanted to continue the
interview he had to say so, that is, that he wanted to continue

the interview now without a lawyer present, and that he had to initiate it as the Agents could not continue. ROUSE then stated, "I want to continue without a lawyer." ROUSE then indicated he wanted to talk to just one of the Agents. He indicated it would be easier for him to speak with only one person rather than two interviewing Agents. Agent WILLIAM VAN ROE elected to leave the interview room. At 5:30 p.m. ROUSE asked to use the rest room and he was allowed to do so. It should be noted that ROUSE could be heard vomiting in an adjacent rest room. He returned to the interview room at 5:36 p.m.

In that ROUSE had wavered several times on whether he wanted an attorney or whether he wanted to continue the interview at the present time, ROUSE was again advised of his rights as they appear on an Interrogation; Advice of Rights form. The form was again read aloud to him while he followed along, reading on the form. ROUSE indicated he wished to continue the interview and provide information. He subsequently signed the Waiver of Rights portion of the form and the interview then proceeded.

When asked to go ahead and say whatever he wanted to concerning this matter, ROUSE just sat in his chair. He then remarked several times, "I don't know" and "I don't know what happened." Upon further questioning, ROUSE then claimed that he had never touched any child in the groin area. He denied ever having sexual intercourse with any children in his mother's house. Further, he denied ever tying anyone up with rope. ROUSE reiterated that he drank a lot, played cards, and partied in the kitchen area of his mother's house.

ROUSE admitted he does smoke marijuana. Asked if some of the children also smoked marijuana with him, ROUSE replied, "Yes." Asked who he smoked dope with, that is, which of the children, ROUSE stated, "My nephew MOSES, MELANIE, THRISTA, that's all." ROUSE then continued, "Oh, JEROME once in awhile." He indicated he had smoked marijuana with those children a couple of months ago in ROSEMARY ROUSE's house.

Questioned as to whether there was any rope in the ROUSE residence, ROUSE indicated there was a white rope in the basement. He indicated the rope was used for a clothesline. ROUSE claimed he had never put any children in a closet, nor locked any of the children in a closet. ROUSE was questioned again as to what he wanted to say, in that he had asked to

198F-MP-39729

Continuation of FD-302 of __DESMOND BENEDICT ROUSE_____ , On __1/25/94___ , Page __4__

continue the interview. He continued to just sit in his chair
and had nothing to say. At 5:51 p.m. Agent PRITCHARD terminated
the interview and no further questions were asked of ROUSE. He
was subsequently furnished a ride from the sheriff's office back
to CLEO TAIL's house, arriving there at approximately 6:00 p.m.

      The following descriptive information was obtained
through interview:

Name	DESMOND BENEDICT ROUSE
	Also known as Dez Rouse
Sex	Male
Race	American Indian
Date of Birth	September 5, 1964
Place of Birth	Wagner, South Dakota
Social Security Number	503-76-4963
Address	Box 101, Marty, South Dakota (currently staying at his cousin CLEO TAIL's house, Lake Andes, South Dakota)
Employment	None
Education	Ninth grade, plus General Equivalency Diploma (GED) in 1984
Military Service	None

- 1 -

FEDERAL BUREAU OF INVESTIGATION

Date of transcription   1/28/94

JESSE LEANDER ROUSE, male American Indian, date of birth May 16, 1959, was contacted at House #515, East Marty Housing, Marty, South Dakota, at the residence of BEATA ROUSE. He was advised of the identity of the interviewing Agent and nature of the interview. It should be noted that the interview took place in an FBI vehicle in the driveway, as there were numerous individuals inside the house.

At the outset of the interview, at 9:06 a.m., ROUSE was advised that he was not under arrest and that the FBI had no intention of arresting him at the conclusion of the interview. Further, he was advised that he did not have to answer any questions, and that if he chose to participate in the interview he could terminate it at any time. He was advised that he was free to leave at any time, and he indicated he understood those facts. ROUSE advised he was sober and was not under the influence of any drugs or medications. He advised he had taken Ibuprofen yesterday, on January 24, 1994, in that he had a sore throat and headache. He advised he was feeling well and that English was his best language. To ensure that ROUSE understood his rights, he was then advised of his rights as they appear on an Interrogation; Advice of Rights form. The form was read aloud to him while he followed along reading on the form. ROUSE indicated he would be willing to participate in an interview, and following the reading of the Waiver of Rights portion of the form, ROUSE signed the Waiver of Rights and the interview then proceeded.

ROUSE indicated he had been living with his sister BEATA ROUSE, at her residence, #515, East Marty Housing, for about two or three weeks. He advised prior to that he lived with his mother ROSEMARY ROUSE, at House #512, East Marty Housing. ROUSE advised that he had returned to the Marty, South Dakota, area in September, 1993, and lived with his mother from that time until his recent move to BEATA ROUSE's residence. ROUSE advised that prior to returning to Marty, South Dakota, in September, 1993, he resided in Wyoming. ROUSE advised he had lived there since 1985.

Investigation on __1/25/94__ at __Marty, South Dakota__ File # __198F-MP-39729__

by __SA PAUL S. PRITCHARD:phs__ Date dictated __1/25/94__

ROUSE was then again advised of the nature of the interview, that being to question him concerning his alleged sexual abuse of numerous children in the ROSEMARY ROUSE residence. ROUSE was questioned concerning any sexual contact he may have had with children in that home. ROUSE explained that he hugs and kisses his own children, whom he identified as MELANIE, MOSES, TABETHA, and CHRISTOPHER. ROUSE advised he was "never with those (other) kids."

ROUSE stated that he slept downstairs in his mother's house and only came up to use the bathroom. He advised that he would urinate in a drainage pipe downstairs, and only went upstairs if it was necessary to use the toilet. ROUSE indicated he lived downstairs until his girlfriend LORI SMITH, broke her leg, at which time they moved upstairs. He indicated she broke her leg the "day before New Years," meaning December 31, 1993, or thereabouts. He advised she broke her leg in an automobile wreck. ROUSE advised that his daughter MELANIE, had a bedroom upstairs at ROSEMARY ROUSE's house. ROUSE indicated he did not spend a lot of time upstairs, other than sometimes playing cards with his mother, and drinking.

ROUSE advised he had moved to BEATA ROUSE's house a couple of weeks ago "to keep our kids." ROUSE explained that Bureau of Indian Affairs (BIA) Criminal Investigator DAN HUDSPETH and Social Worker JEAN BROCK told ROUSE that ROSEMARY ROUSE's residence was an "unsafe environment." Asked why it was deemed an unsafe environment, ROUSE replied, "Cause DEZ and GARFIELD was up there." He indicated he was referring to DESMOND ROUSE and GARFIELD FEATHER. ROUSE advised that there were "always kids around" at his mother's house.

ROUSE was then questioned, specifically, concerning his alleged sexual abuse of THRISTA ROUSE. Asked if he ever kissed her, ROUSE replied, "No." He indicated THRISTA was his niece in that she is URSULA's daughter. URSULA is JESSE ROUSE's sister and is also named URSULA ROUSE. Asked why he had never given his own niece a kiss, ROUSE replied, "Well, I give her a kiss on the cheek once in awhile." ROUSE denied ever touching her breasts or groin area. Further, he claimed he had never had sexual intercourse with her, answering "No" when questioned about that. ROUSE was asked if he ever tied THRISTA ROUSE up, and he replied, "No, never." He indicated he had not tied her up even when playing with her.

198F-MP-39729

Continuation of FD-302 of ___JESSE LEANDER ROUSE_____ , On ___1/25/94___ , Page ___3___

     ROUSE was questioned as to whether he had ever put some of the children or locked some of the children in a closet in ROSEMARY ROUSE's house. ROUSE stated, "Never did put them in the closet." ROUSE then stated that there "are closets upstairs, but none of them have doors on them." He explained that the bedroom closets do not have doors, though he added he was not sure if the closet in URSULA's room had a door. ROUSE indicated there were two closet doors in the hallway upstairs, that served as a pantry and linen closet, that had doors. He reiterated that he did not know if URSULA's closet had a door, in that she kept a lock on her bedroom door. ROUSE advised his daughter MELANIE's room does not have a closet door. Further, he indicated the spare bedroom does not have a closet door.

     ROUSE advised that MELANIE shared a room with TABETHA, MOSES, and CHRISTOPHER. He indicated a second bedroom was a spare room which was used by the children to play Nintendo in. He advised the third bedroom was used by URSULA and two children: ECHO and THRISTA. ROUSE advised his mother slept in the living room, along with DERRICK, ROSEMARY ROUSE, and CHRISTOPHER. ROUSE advised that he, DESMOND ROUSE, and GARFIELD FEATHER all stayed downstairs.

     ROUSE advised that BEATA ROUSE had her five children staying with her. He identified them as FURY ROUSE, JEROME ROUSE, DONOVAN ROUSE, JESSICA ROUSE, and LUCRITIA ROUSE.

     ROUSE was then questioned concerning any sexual contact or activities he may have had with LUCRITIA. He explained he had never touched her in a sexual abusive manner, that is, had never touched her in the groin area. Further, he indicated he had never engaged in any sexual acts with her.

     ROUSE was then questioned as to whether he smoked marijuana in his mother's house, to which he replied, "Yeah," that he did. He acknowledged that he knew that was illegal. ROUSE advised that he also drank a lot. Further, he stated that GARFIELD FEATHER, DESMOND ROUSE, his mother (ROSEMARY ROUSE), DWAYNE ROUSE, and RUSSELL HUBBLING also drank a lot.

     ROUSE was then questioned further concerning his alleged sexual contact with children in the ROUSE home. ROUSE stated, "If I did I must have been pretty drunk." He continued, "Sorry if it happened, but if it did I was drunk." ROUSE

Continuation of FD-302 of __JESSE LEANDER ROUSE__ , On __1/25/94__ , Page __4__

advised, "I just can't remember doing anything like that." ROUSE advised that the children involved, including LUCRITIA, THRISTA, and others residing in his home, all loved him and cared about him. Further, ROUSE advised that he also loved and cared about the children. ROUSE could offer no explanation as to why the children, whom he indicated love him and whom he also loves, would make such allegations against him, if they were not true.

ROUSE advised that DESMOND ROUSE "likes to party." He advised that DESMOND likes to joke around with the children and tease them, by calling them nicknames. ROUSE claimed not to have participated in any sexual activity with any juveniles while with DESMOND. ROUSE explained that he and DESMOND usually get out of their mother's house by about 9:30 a.m. and return back to her home about 4:30 p.m., "after the kids get home from school. And we drink." ROUSE reiterated, with regard to his alleged sexual activity with children, that none ever happened "that I know of." ROUSE advised, with regard to GARFIELD FEATHER, that FEATHER "drinks a few beers and passes out. That's all I know about him."

ROUSE was questioned as to whether he would be willing to take a polygraph examination concerning this matter, and he agreed to take a polygraph at some future date.

At 11:48 a.m. the interview was concluded and ROUSE left the Bureau vehicle, unescorted, and returned to BEATA ROUSE's residence.

The following information was obtained through observation and interview:

Name	JESSE LEANDER ROUSE
Sex	Male
Race	American Indian
Date of Birth	May 16, 1959
Place of Birth	Wagner, South Dakota
Social Security Number	503-76-4918
Address	House #515, East Marty Housing Marty, South Dakota (home of his sister BEATA ROUSE)
Prior Addresses	(1) #512, East Marty Housing, Marty, South Dakota (home of his mother ROSEMARY ROUSE)

Continuation of FD-302 of JESSE LEANDER ROUSE _____ , On __1/25/94__ , Page __5__

	(2) 941 South Melrose, Casper, Wyoming 82601
Education	High school graduate, Marty Indian School, Marty, South Dakota
Prior Military Service	None
Drivers License	Wyoming, #103497-079C
Height	6'2"
Weight	260 pounds
Eyes	Brown
Hair	Brown
Employment	Wood cutting crew for Yankton Sioux Tribe
Prior Employment	Worked for JOHN BROWN COMPANY on a contract with NAVAL PETROLEUM RESERVE, Wyoming
Children	Four: MELANIE, MOSES, TABETHA, and CHRISTOPHER

D-302 (Rev. 3-10-82)

FEDERAL BUREAU OF INVESTIGATION

Date of transcription _____3/30/94_____

JESSICA ROUSE appeared at the office of the United States Attorney, Sioux Falls, South Dakota, and in the presence of Special Agent (SA) WILLIAM VAN ROE and Assistant United States Attorney (AUSA) MICHELLE TAPKEN. She appeared in the United States Attorney's Office to clarify what she had said about her uncles in an earlier interview. ROUSE advised that JESSE ROUSE touched her with his hand where she pees. JESSE also put his "private spot" into her where she pees. JESSE also put his "private spot" in her where she poops.

DESMOND ROUSE touched her "private spot" with his hand. DESMOND also put his "private spot" in her in her front and back. He also put his finger into her butt.

Investigation on ___3/21/94___ at _Sioux Falls, SD___ File # _198F-MP-39729_

by _SA WILLIAM VAN ROE:smi_ Date dictated _3/24/94_

FD-302 (Rev. 3-10-82)

FEDERAL BUREAU OF INVESTIGATION

Date of transcription   3/30/94

LICRETIA ROUSE appeared at the United States Attorney's Office to clarify statements that she made earlier concerning her uncles. She was interviewed in the presence of Special Agent (SA) WILLIAM VAN ROE of the FBI, and Assistant United States Attorney (AUSA) MICHELLE TAPKEN. She advised that JESSE ROUSE put his finger in her where she pees. He also put his "private spot" in her where she pees and poops. JESSE also threatened her.

RUSSELL HUBBELING, GARFIELD FEATHER, DESMOND ROUSE, and JESSE ROUSE all put their "private spots" in her where she pees.

RUSSELL HUBBELING tied her up on the bed and put ashes in her mouth. He also put his "private spot" in her "front."

GARFIELD FEATHER put his "private spot" into her "private spot" where she pees. He also slapped her.

DESMOND ROUSE tied her up on the bed and took her clothes off. He got on top of her and put his "private spot" in her. He put his finger in her where she pees. He also cut her on the head with a knife when he threw the knife at her because he was made because she was watching television.

Investigation on   3/21/94   at Sioux Falls, SD   File #   198F-MP-39729

by   SA WILLIAM VAN ROE:smi   Date dictated   3/24/94

smoking "dope" and described the dope as a "tobacco substance and it goes into pipes." The night of the incident that she described with LICREATIA, people were drinking beer and smoking pipes.

Her grandmother ROSEMARY does not drink and her Aunt URSULA does not drink.

She explained that her Uncle DESMOND spanks kids when he is mad. He usually does the spanking when he is drinking and he uses a belt.

She explained that her Uncle GARFIELD puts his "pee-pee" in her "private spot." HUDSPETH showed ROSEMARY a drawing of a young man. The young man's penis was explained to ROSEMARY at which time she said her "private spot" is in the same place as the boy's penis, but is different.

She recalled that Uncle GARFIELD put his "private part" in her "private part" in her front and also in her back and that when he did this to her it felt bad. She believes that Uncle GARFIELD's "private spot" was soft when he did this to her. This incident occurred in her grandmother's bedroom or in URSULA's bedroom in the back of her grandmother's residence.

She recalled that Uncle GARFIELD did this to her "a lot of times" and that she could not recall the first or the last time.

She did recall that Uncle GARFIELD tied her up to the bed with ropes and that the ropes were yellow and that he got the ropes from outside and brought them into the house. GARFIELD tied her hands out away from her body and she was on the bed on her back and her feet were also tied apart. She was alone and GARFIELD kissed her on the lips. GARFIELD had his clothes off and she had her clothes on and she tried or would not let him take her clothes off. She recalled that he went up and down on her and that he tried to put his "private part" in hers. She recalled being on her back and that she was tied to the bed and she thought his "private part" was soft while he was doing this to her, but recalled it hurt when he touched her private parts. She recalled that this incident occurred in the daytime. She also recalled that everyone had left the residence except she and GARFIELD, and that the other members of the family had gone to

ontinuation of FD-302 of ___ROSEMARY ROUSE, II_____ , On ___1/19/94___ , Page ___3___

church in Marty, South Dakota, and that was in the summertime.
She also explained that she had been at her grandmother's for a
period of time before this incident occurred and it was before
she went to DONNA JORDAN's to stay.

She recalled that GARFIELD also tied up LICREATIA and
JESSICA the same way that he had tied her up. She saw what
happened and explained that GARFIELD took their clothes off and
got on top of them at grandmother's house. She could not recall
the exact room, but explained that it was a bedroom and that
ROSEMARY was in the room. When this incident occurred, GARFIELD
was alone with the children and was babysitting them. The rest
of the family had gone to church. This incident with LICREATIA
and JESSICA occurred before he had done the same thing to her
when she was alone with GARFIELD. She believes that both
incidents occurred approximately one week apart.

She also recalled that GARFIELD took his hands and
touched her in her "private parts" and explained that he used his
finger, which was determined to be the index finger of his hand,
and put it in her "private spot." She recalled that when he did
that it hurt and she cried. GARFIELD stopped doing that to her
after she cried, but it took him a long time to stop doing this.

In regard to LICREATIA and JESSICA, she recalled that
GARFIELD got on top of them and laid on top of each one of them.
GARFIELD grabbed his "private part" and put it in their "private
spots" in their back or butt at which time they both would cry.
She was tied up at the time as well, but on this occasion
GARFIELD did not do anything to her.

- 1 -

FEDERAL BUREAU OF INVESTIGATION

Date of transcription ___4/6/94___

      JESSE LEANDER ROUSE, was interviewed at the Charles Mix County Jail, Lake Andes, South Dakota, where he was temporarily being detained and under arrest for Aggravated Sexual Abuse charges. ROUSE was told the names of the interviewing Agents and the nature of the interview and was presented one copy of an Interrogation; Advice of Rights form which Special Agent (SA) VAN ROE read aloud to him. After completion of the reading of form, ROUSE stated he understood his rights as read and signed the waiver portion of the form, but pointed out that he would not answer any questions concerning the charges that he was currently under arrest for. The interview was immediately terminated.

Investigation on ___3/30/94___ at ___Lake Andes, SD___ File # ___198F-MP-39729___

    SA ALFRED D. BRAMUCCI
by ___SA WILLIAM VAN ROE:smi___ Date dictated ___3/31/94___

- 1 -

FEDERAL BUREAU OF INVESTIGATION

Date of transcription _____4/7/94_____

        This is to record the fact that JESSE LEANDER ROUSE,
male Native American, date of birth May 16, 1959, Social Security
Account Number 503-76-4918, was placed under Federal custody by
Special Agent (SA) DREW C. MC CONAGHY and SA STEVEN L. SCHLOBOHM
at the Tribal Hall in Marty, South Dakota, on the Yankton Sioux
Indian Reservation.

        At approximately 8:50 a.m., SAs MC CONAGHY and
SCHLOBOHM entered the Tribal Hall and requested to speak with
JESSE ROUSE, who had checked in for work as a wood cutter at the
hall at approximately 7:56 a.m. After repeated attempts to page
JESSE ROUSE to the front entryway, SAs MC CONAGHY and SCHLOBOHM
went downstairs, toward the kitchen area, where JESSE ROUSE was
found as he was attempting to leave through a back door.

        At that time, SAs MC CONAGHY and SCHLOBOHM escorted
ROUSE out through the front door of the Tribal Hall into the
street, where he was searched, handcuffed, and placed into the
front seat of the Bureau car.

        ROUSE was given the opportunity to briefly speak with
his girlfriend, LAURA (last name unknown), so that arrangements
could be made to take care of the children in her custody. ROUSE
was then transported to the Charles Mix County Sheriff's Office
where he was fingerprinted, photographed, and lodged until
transportation to Sioux Falls, South Dakota, could be arranged.

        ROUSE was subsequently transported to Sioux Falls,
South Dakota, where an initial appearance was held before the
United States Magistrate.

Investigation on __3/30/94__ at _Marty, South Dakota_ File # _198F-MP-39729_

        SA STEVEN L. SCHLOBOHM
by _SA DREW C. MC CONAGHY:DCM:phs_____ Date dictated _4/1/94_

-1-

FEDERAL BUREAU OF INVESTIGATION

Date of transcription   4/6/94

DUANE MICHAEL ROUSE was arrested at the Security Office of the United Tribes Technical Education Center at 8:20 a.m.

He was then advised of the charges and provided copies of the indictment and arrest warrant. He said that he did not want to further discuss the matter.

ROUSE acknowledged that his name, date of birth, place of birth and tribal enrolment were correct as recorded on an FD-302 interview dated March 8, 1994. ROUSE said that the Social Security Account Number was incorrectly reported. That number should be 503-76-4940.

After a security officer brought ROUSE a jacket, he was transported to the United States Marshal's Office where he was processed and met with Pretrial Services. He then appeared before a Federal Magistrate Judge for a scheduled 11:15 am. initial appearance.

Investigation on __3/30/94__ at __Bismarck, ND__ File # __198F-MP-39729__

by __SA RICHARD K. FUHRMAN and__
__SA CRAIG R. WELKEN__   CRW:jlb   Date dictated __3/30/94__

FD-302 (Rev. 3-10-82)

- 1 -

FEDERAL BUREAU OF INVESTIGATION

Date of transcription   3/14/94

       DUANE MICHAEL ROUSE was contacted at the Campus Security Office at the United Tribes Educational Technical Center, 3315 University Drive, Bismarck, North Dakota 58504.

       ROUSE arrived at the security office on foot after Security Officer FRANK BRAVEBULL requested a dormitory staff member to ask ROUSE to come to the office.

       ROUSE was introduced to the interviewing Agent through the display of official FBI credentials. He was advised that he was not then nor would he be at the conclusion of the interview under arrest that day. He was told that he was free to leave at any time, that he did not have to speak with the interviewing Agent and that it was a voluntary interview. ROUSE indicated that he understood but was willing to proceed.

       ROUSE provided the following descriptive data about himself:

Name:	DUANE MICHAEL ROUSE
Race:	Indian
Sex:	Male
Tribal Enrollment:	Yankton Sioux Tribe
Date of Birth:	February 7, 1962
Place of Birth:	Wagner, South Dakota
Social Security Account Number:	503-76-4970
Height:	5'11"
Weight:	189 pounds
Hair:	Dark brown
Eyes:	Brown
Current Residence:	Sitting Bull Hall
Permanent Residence:	Box 244 Marty, South Dakota 57361

Investigation on   3/8/94   at Bismarck, ND   File # 198F-MP-39729

by   SA CRAIG R. WELKEN:jlb   Date dictated 3/8/94

| Educational Program: | Three semester welding course, currently enrolled in the first semester which began in January, 1994 |
| Prior Employment: | Change Person Tribal Casino |

ROUSE said he had no idea why the interviewing Agent desired to speak with him. He was advised there had been allegations that he had touched young children in their private areas. He immediately responded that he had never done such a thing, although he had spanked children for disciplinary reasons.

ROUSE acknowledged there were liquor parties held in various houses in Marty, South Dakota, but he did not know of any children who were improperly touched during those occasions.

Further, he had no reason why the children who made allegations would be lying.

ROUSE has five children, four sons and a daughter, who stay with his mother-in-law, SHIRLEY BLACKSMITH of Marty, South Dakota. They are TIMOTHY, age 12, THOMAS, age 10, DUANE, age 5, RODRICK, also known as R.J., age 4, and RIO, age 4. RODRICK and RIO are twins.

ROUSE's family seems to have a number of arguments, but he does not feel that would lead to allegations about improperly touching children.

ROUSE's mother, ROSEMARY ROUSE, last contacted him in February or March. He received a letter from her wherein she sent his income tax materials and said everything was okay in Marty. He has two brothers and one sister. He has a brother with four children and a sister with one child who live with his mother. Another sister, BEATA ROUSE, approximately 30 years old, has five children. BEATA does not live with his mother but does live in the same housing development. BEATA did live with his mother until several months ago.

LUCRETRIA ROUSE is his sister BEATA's child. She is approximately five years old. His only contact with her would have been during visits to BEATA's house.

ROUSE has been at BEATA's house a few times to visit, perhaps only four to five times since she moved to her current residence. He was there on one or two occasions when there were parties. He does not get along with his sister, so he does not spend that much time with her.

DESMOND ROUSE is his younger brother. He has never been to BEATA's house with DESMOND. However, the two men were present at the same time that BEATA's children resided at ROSEMARY's house.

When DUANE goes back to the reservation he usually stays at SHIRLEY BLACKSMITH's house. The last visit to his mother's home in Wagner was during the last week of December, 1993, he did not stay overnight. He also visited his mother's home a couple of times during December prior to that last week. He usually visited during the daytime, but he was also there watching television between the hours of 8:00 to 9:00 p.m.

ROUSE denied hearing allegations that his brothers had improperly touched young children. He said that he knows a lot of drinking of whiskey had gone on at his mother's house and had been there during some of those occasions but did not participate in improper touching of children, nor did he know of such contacts by any other person.

All of the children in his family and his sister's family get along well with him. He had no knowledge of any of them being locked up or in any other ways mistreated.

ROUSE could not explain why he did not get along well with his sister, he said it just did not work out with them over the long haul. He does not believe that her children would tell lies.

ROUSE said that on his honor he had never touched the children improperly.

ROUSE was only aware of one child who was taken away from his mother, and that was done during November or December, 1993. That related to an incident where there was an alleged spanking and the child was not being fed properly. That child's name was ROSEMARY. The mother resided in Montana.

FD-302a (Rev. 11-15-83)

198F-MP-39729

ROUSE had no further information that would help in the investigation.

ROUSE did not want to take a polygraph examination because he did not believe he would do well on one. He would not give further consideration in taking it, and his final answer was no. He is not worried about what his reputation is in the community.

ROUSE has a criminal record in tribal court which would have a variety of tribal charges, perhaps as many as 20. The charges include disorderly conduct, resisting arrest and other offenses primarily related to alcohol abuse.

ROUSE was also arrested as a minor when he was 11 years old on a state charge of stealing some items from a car. That matter was handled in Yankton.

ROUSE believes he will be expelled from the United Tribes Educational Technical Center in about a week for alcohol abuse. He said he has tried treatment in the past, and it does not help. He said there is too much peer pressure for him to resist it.

He asked if it was okay for him to call back to inquire about the situation at home. He was advised that there were no restrictions being placed on him other than he should not in any way attempt to threaten any victims or witnesses. He acknowledged that he understood that.